Evangelism and Learning Disability

Learning from the Faith and Light Communities

Capt Alan Lowe, Church Army

Lay Trainer in Evangelism, West Bromwich Deanery

GROVE BOOKS LIMITED
RIDLEY HALL RD CAMBRIDGE. CB3 9HU

Contents

Acknowledgements

Thanks to my family: to Mary for her love and support; to James for inspiring me to write; to Kevin and Helen for making me feel proud.

The Cover Illustration is by Meb who himself has Down's syndrome.

Church Army and the Grove Evangelism Series

Church Army has over 350 evangelists working in five areas of focus, at the cutting edge of evangelism in the UK. It co-sponsors the publication of the Grove Evangelism Series as part of its aim of stimulating discussion about evangelism strategies, and sharing its experience of front-line evangelism.

Further details about Church Army are available from:
Church Army, Independents Road, Blackheath, London SE3 9LG.
Telephone: 0181 318 1226. Fax: 0181 318 5258.
Registered charity number: 226226

First Impression May 1998
ISSN 1367-0840
ISBN 1 85174 373 1

1

Introduction

James is fifteen years old. He has no recognizable speech and only a very short memory span. He needs constant supervision and help with the most basic activities. He may well do anything at any given moment.

One Sunday morning James and I went to church together. There was just the two of us because mum was in bed ill. He was in a rather quiet mood on this occasion, except when we sang. During each hymn he turned to face me, and holding my arms began to dance. All around us sombre faces began to develop infectious smiles.

As far as I am aware James did not understand a word of those hymns. I doubt very much whether he would have appreciated the skills of the organist, or the theology of worship either. But it seems to me that James encountered the living God, and communicated that as only he could.

My first marriage was to a woman who died prematurely as a result of having muscular dystrophy. Thus I already had experience of living alongside long-term disability before marrying my lovely wife Mary. Her son James has very severe learning disabilities, needing one-to-one care. These experiences have focused for me how God wants to be involved in all aspects of our lives, including the brokenness. However, it is in the area of learning disability that my own thinking has recently been challenged. Contemporary society has begun to get its act together with regard to its caring responsibilities for such people. But what of their spiritual development, which is the local church's responsibility. Is it enough for us as Christ's spokespersons, to see them simply as pastoral concerns? Are they as human persons any less needy of nurturing their relationship with God? Unless the answer to both these questions is 'yes,' which I would suggest is naïve, then they need to hear the gospel message too.

This investigation is an attempt to highlight good practice for evangelism among those with significant learning disabilities, or what used to be known as mental handicap. For clarification learning disability is different from mental illness in that it is the person's natural condition.[1] The latter is potentially correctable by drugs, therapy or time. Because the real handicap of those with severe learning disabilities is in grappling with intellectual concepts, it would be inappropriate to focus on theory alone. Therefore I am working 'bottom up' by looking at some current Christian work in this area and allowing positive aspects of that to inform good practice.

During my investigations I became aware of a parallel issue. Those with

---

1   I am not happy with the term 'learning disability' because it does not describe the situation fully. However, I have generally used the term because it is currently considered the most appropriate by those who work in this field.

learning disability express their humanity and spirituality in ways which often by-pass reason alone. This is precisely the way our postmodern culture is moving. What becomes clear is that in thinking through evangelism with this particular group, valuable insights are gained for evangelism more generally. The piece of work which I have experienced and investigated is a worldwide movement known as 'Faith and Light.'

2

Small Beginnings:
A Short History of 'Faith and Light'

'Another parable he put before them, saying, "The Kingdom of Heaven is like a grain of mustard seed which a man took and sowed in his field; it is the smallest of all the seeds, but when it has grown it is the greatest of shrubs and becomes a tree, so that the birds of the air come and make nests in its branches."'

Matthew 13.31-32

A Family's Pain

The inspiration for Faith and Light (F&L) grew out of the pain of a French family. Loic and Thaddee were two young boys with profound intellectual disabilities, whose parents, Camille and Gerard, wanted to take them to Lourdes. There was, however, no room for them on the Diocesan Pilgrimage for reasons such as, 'They are too disabled' and 'They won't understand anything' or 'They will upset the others.'[2] The couple organized their own trip to Lourdes, but this turned out to be a painful experience too. Rudely treated at the hotel, they were served their meals in their room to spare the other guests discomfort, and suffered such comments as 'Children like that should be left at home.' But their pain turned out to be a catalyst for a whole new movement of the gospel.

Meeting a Greater Need

F&L evolved gradually but one particular meeting was vital in its beginnings. Marie Helene Mathieu knew the family and was touched by the, 'Suffering of the parents and their desire for their children to be integrated into society and church life.' Jean Vanier, an ex naval officer and a graduate in philosophy, had started the first L'Arche community four years earlier.[3] For three of those four years he had

---

2 *The Seed and the Tree* (Faith and Light Secretariat, 1995) p 50.
3 L'Arche are residential communities for people with learning disabilities.

4

taken severely learning disabled men on pilgrimages, which had been very beneficial in helping the community develop. Their conversation in a car somewhere between Compiegne and Paris, focused a vision for a huge pilgrimage. It was to be for people with learning disabilities, and their parents, carers and friends. 'All things are possible for God' (Matthew 19.26) became the prime words of encouragement as they set out on this risky undertaking. Three years of planning in small groups began focusing on spiritual preparation, liturgy, and the immense practicalities of it all. At the time this was very pioneering, but a venture which exceeded expectations.

A Good Friday

In a F&L publication to mark its fifteenth anniversary (1984) Marie tells of that first pilgrimage—how on Good Friday 1971 there were 12,000 people at the Massabielle grotto in Lourdes, Southern France, of whom 4,000 had a learning disability. The response of local Lourdes people seemed to move on from initial fear, to surprise and finally to welcome. Clearly it was not only those with learning disabilities that were being enriched through that unique Easter weekend.

At the end of that weekend the corporate desire was that, 'something must continue.' Jean Vanier's response was a call to those present to, 'do whatever the Holy Spirit inspires you to do to build a world of love around the handicapped person.'[4] Thus some of those small preparation communities continued meeting, and some flourished. The movement continued to develop at a steady pace, although its early fragmentation and informal structure make details of these early years difficult to clarify. What is certain is that the early communities varied considerably from festivals for 2-3,000 people to small prayer groups. Eventually years of planning and discussion resulted in an international charter for F&L, agreed at a meeting in England.

The movement has gone from strength to strength. In 1995 there were an estimated 1,276 affiliated communities worldwide, covering all the continents. Regional, national and international bodies meet for prayerful planning and celebration, organizing holidays, camps and retreats. A specific ethos for meetings has also developed which structures gatherings into a three-stage process (see next chapter).

F&L is ecumenical, and all of the main Christian Churches are represented within it, though the majority of groups are Roman Catholic, reflecting its origins. Like many ecumenical bodies they have had their struggles, but generally have moved forward quite positively. Perhaps the lack of partisanship expressed by those with learning disabilities has helped. My first-hand investigation of F&L included attending regional gatherings, meetings with leaders and attending local F&L communities—specifically those of Southwell/Halam and Rainworth groups in Nottinghamshire, Seacroft in Leeds, and the Sheffield and Hallam communities in Sheffield. My observations and experiences follow.

---

4 *The Seed and the Tree*, p 71.

3

Faith and Light:
Its Purpose and Practice

'"The kingdom of heaven is like yeast that a woman took and mixed in with three measures of flour until all of it was leavened." Jesus told the crowds all these things in parables; without a parable he told them nothing. This was to fulfil what had been spoken through the prophet: "I will open my mouth to speak in parables; I will proclaim what has been hidden from the foundation of the world."'

Matthew 13.33-34

F&L meetings vary according to the context, but all generally follow a three-fold structure of Welcome, Prayer and Celebration.

Welcome (and Sharing)

I experienced a warm welcome at most of the groups. Leaders made a point of introducing visitors, such as myself, sensitively. Some of the learning disabled folk uninhibitedly speak to visitors as though they have known them for years! At Rainworth, Michael, who has limited coordination and speech, approached me as soon as I arrived. 'Hello what's your name?' he said, offering me his hand. By simply being himself, he gave me the opportunity to announce early on that 'I am Alan from Sheffield.'

Names are important in F&L, where one's status is less so. The name is the person and group leaders work hard to know everyone's name and use it properly. At Rainworth, Marilyn led us in a kind of Eucharistic Peace. She took everyone by the hand and looked them in the eye. As she did so she assured them by name and with conviction that they were loved by Jesus.

At Halam on 14th February we made big hearts on to which everyone else stuck a small heart. During the process I heard things like, 'This heart is for you,' 'This is because you are special,' and 'God likes you!' Derek, in his forties with Down's syndrome, beamed as he placed his heart on mine. In the midst of the St Valentine's day commercializing and sentimentalizing, I experienced a love more about openness and respect. It was powerful in its simplicity. Jean Vanier has talked about real caring as, 'Being transformed into Jesus, loving others and giving ourselves to them.'[5]

The sharing time varies but is often a craft activity or a rôle-play or drama relating to a Bible story. The Good Samaritan was a memorable one. Jackie, with significant learning disabilities, was my partner. Imagining we were injured we bandaged one another's hands, before feeding each other. For Jackie and others

---

5 *The Spirituality of F&L*, p 6. (details)

with learning disabilities this was easy because they were not really acting, just being themselves in caring.

Any leader in parish ministry knows that welcoming environments do not just happen! Generally F&L leaders saw their roles as pioneers in this. Malcolm (Hallamshire), Geoff and Marilyn (Rainworth), Bob (Leeds), and Liz (Newark) are very different characters. All, however, are clearly committed to F&L's philosophy for creating community. At a planning meeting for the new Hallamshire group there were an amazing 20 potential helpers. They were willing to do 'anything' to make the group 'work for the disabled.' The commitment was humbling, the determination inspiring, and the open agenda a relief!

Prayer

The most striking aspect of F&L is the integration of prayer into its activities. Those with learning disabilities tend to have a less compartmentalized view of life, and prayer cannot just be a separate activity. In a prayer time at Halam, Helen, with moderate to severe learning disabilities, danced spontaneously. In that particular moment she seemed to sum up the mood of the group, and communicated God's presence with us in a very visual way. There were hands held and shoulders gently touched in prayerful moments. David, with Down's syndrome, spontaneously venerated the cross during a meeting in Holy week! He did however have problems coping with Jesus' death. Whenever the crucifixion was mentioned David burst into tears shouting 'no!,' as though he could change the fact. Geoff, as leader, carried on relating Jesus' suffering unperturbed and when Easter Sunday was mentioned David's smile was huge! He really had relived Jesus' suffering and joy with him. Life is a mixture of joy and sadness and I was impressed by F&L's resistance to sheltering the learning disabled from the latter. I also understood more fully the word *anamnesis*.[6]

The smaller groups discussed specifically what to pray for, the discussion being a major part of the prayer! There were tears and grumbles when Sue, who had left the group to work in Pakistan, was prayed for. Kenneth, with Down's syndrome, beamed at me when someone prayed for me and my work. Derek, also with Down's syndrome, whose mum had died some months before, spontaneously burst into tears. Thanksgiving prayers for things like the spring flowers or Debra's new baby niece produced a sense of delight and wonder. I found this calming, as I often arrived in the middle of a schedule. Jesus was frequently mentioned by name or signed in Makaton, a simplified sign language often used during praying and singing.[7] This is quite moving as it means that prayers are heard *and* seen. I was certainly moved to tears at a regional gathering in Leeds as people struggled forward on crutches or were led up to voice their prayers. One very

---

6   NT Greek word for remembrance. Literally to make something 'a present reality.' See Luke 22.19.
7   Makaton is a sign language for people with limited communication. It is a simplified form of a deaf sign language.

uncoordinated young man leapt up sending the microphone flying and many more were desperate to publicly say their prayers to God. One lady, almost inaudible, seemed to pray, 'God, thank you for being God. Amen.'

Celebration (and the Meal)

Eleven years of Christian faith has taken me from ten and a half stones in weight to nearly thirteen! Food is always on the agenda at the meetings, although it is usually simple. I enjoyed sausage roll and cake on one occasion, and bread and cheese with a fruit juice on another. The 'meal' I shared in at my first visit to the Rainworth group left me with a really positive impression. Only after reflecting on this did I realize why, and appreciate the care behind it. Attractive table cloths, flowers, serviettes and carefully presented food had all touched my senses. Smelling, touching, tasting, hearing and seeing had all subconsciously formed part of the communication. With some guilt I recalled times when I have produced my step son James' meals in a hurry, forgetting how the experience is about more than filling a stomach!

Conversation takes place during the meal. Sometimes it flows and on other occasions it is a struggle. When there was nothing to say I noticed how for those who are disabled, like Derek and Debra at Halam, Kenneth and Jackie at Rainworth or the learning disabled lady who sat next to me in Sheffield, this was no problem. They were all happy to say nothing if there was nothing to be said! Raymond from Leeds, having never met me before, had no problems conversing though. He excitedly gave me all the details of his forthcoming holiday, before proceeding to invite me to join him on it! He was sure his care assistants would not mind at all. If only all God's people were so confident in sharing good news! At that same meeting I met representatives of F&L communities in Ireland, Sweden and Norway who were visiting Britain. It really did feel like being in Jerusalem at Pentecost. F&L is conscious of its global calling and works hard at creating cross-cultural gatherings. Following on from a leaders' meeting which they had attended, was an international camp for the learning disabled and their friends. This made it very real to me that I belonged to 'One Holy Catholic and Apostolic church.' I also met people within F&L, from various denominations, and also a good number of unchurched people who belonged to some of the communities too. Elaine was one such person, brought along by her care assistant to the inaugural meeting of the Hallamshire group. She was in a wheelchair and came at the last minute, making a grand entrance. Her speech was only grunts, but her laugh was infectious. When someone tripped over her wheelchair, and when she splattered paint on someone's lap, she just roared with laughter. A number of people, including myself, went home that afternoon having had a really good laugh. I felt as though I had seen Christ himself through the joy of that young lady.

A Proper Perspective

There is actually a fourth element to F&L, which is the time between meetings, known as Bread and Salt. This is all that happens between meetings and where F&L dovetails with the life of the local church. F&L is committed to helping integrate the learning disabled into mainstream church. The Rainworth group works closely with its mother church of St Simon and St Jude. The practice here is one which local churches could learn from, even those where there is currently no formal F&L group or any such group planned.

There is much that is positive to learn from F&L as we seek to evangelize and be evangelized by people with moderate, severe or profound learning disabilities. However F&L is not a community of perfected saints. People being awkward, saying unpleasant things, being made to perform, or showing off to the point of irritation were also part of the life of the groups. As a Roman Catholic priest Marcel Gaudilliere says, 'They fall into sin like the rest of us.'[8] But there is much positive to learn from, and summarized in the following words:

Small things matter	Belonging
Compassion	Shared vulnerability
Relationships/Friendship	A sense of wonder
Christian atmosphere	Struggling for unity
Whole life prayer	Responding to God
Jesus' presence	Acting and role playing truths
Church integration	Cultural relevance
Practical caring	Affirmation
The pain	Communication without words
Greater openness	

---

8   *Deepening our Spirituality* (Faith and Light Secretariat, 1991) p 14.

4

Belonging to Christ:
A Theological Perspective

'While he was still speaking to the crowds, someone told him, "Look, your mother and your brothers are standing outside, wanting to speak to you." But to the one who had told him this, Jesus replied, " Who is my mother and who are my brothers? " And pointing to his disciples, he said, "Here are my mother and my brothers! For whoever does the will of my Father in heaven is my brother and sister and mother."'

Luke 12.46–50

Personhood

'God said, "Let us make humankind in our image, according to our likeness…"' (Genesis 1.26). This phrase is central to informing our concepts of church and evangelism which properly includes those of impaired intellectual abilities. Having focused primarily on reason in the past, contemporary understanding of the *imago dei* is now attempting to be more inclusive. A and R Hansen, in their book *Reasonable Belief*, link the image of God with freedom, in particular with 'creative freedom.'[9] Reason, freedom of expression and creativity are no doubt important components in how people, learning disabled or not, reflect the character of God. However, if being made in the image of our creator is to be 'the foundation for human dignity,' as has been said, it must be fully inclusive.[10] It has to include even the most profoundly disabled person for whom freedom to express themselves creatively and intellectually may be significantly impaired.

A Trinitarian faith helps prioritize the importance of relationships. This is now increasingly being seen as the prime expression of being made in God's likeness. Alastair McFaddyen in *The Call to Personhood* views relationality as two-directional—vertical and horizontal. Vertically, people 'cannot…avoid being in relation to God,' and any freedom we have is in '…determining what form our response, is to take.'[11] God communicates via Spirit, not just grey matter, and those with even the severest learning disabilities are as capable of this vertical relationship as anyone. But the horizontal side of relating, person to person, is closely linked to this. It is here that people with communication limitations are disadvantaged.

Psychology has shown how our experiences shape what we are like. Horizontally, as it were, when we receive affirmation, trust, respect, and freedom to choose

9   A and R Hansen, *Reasonable Belief* (OUP, 1982), p 29.
10 Sinclair Ferguson (ed), *New Dictionary of Theology* (IVP, 1988), p 329.
11 A McFaddyen, *The Call To Personhood* (CUP, 1990), p 24.

we also know how to receive these vertically from God. We are thus enabled to respond in mutual love, obedience and trust. This link means that those who are less disabled need to be pro-active and imaginative in exploring all levels of relationship with those who are more disabled. Otherwise such people's ability to relate to God may well be progressively impaired. This is a conclusion which lacks sentimentality I freely admit!

'All contribute to the image and we are the body of Christ only in mutuality and corporately. The handicapped must contribute to the image and society must see their contribution also.'

Frances Young, *Face to Face* (p 191)

'Scriptures lead very few to faith. Speakers lead very few to faith. Experiences (encounters with others mainly) are the most normative faith-building experiences.'

David Pailin, *A Gentle Touch* (p 131)

No discussion on personhood can ignore the incarnation. The uniting of divinity with humanity in the life of Jesus underlines three important truths. After agreeing to be the mother of the Saviour of the world Mary recognized how his coming would, '...lift up the lowly' (Luke 1.52). We also marvel at how closely the creator chooses to relate to his creation, by becoming flesh and dwelling among us. To God all matter matters, and not just grey matter! And the incarnation encourages us by showing how God desires to communicate as imaginatively as possible with his people. We should attempt no less with one another, even in the more difficult relationships.

Any communication between people promotes creative relationship and a sense of belonging. At fifteen our son James has no speech, aside a possible 'mu-um.' He communicates via behaviour, body language, grunts, looks, touch and also emotions which are transmitted somehow. This 'somehow' communication only develops with time and experience. After five years of knowing him I am just beginning to grasp it, whereas his mother has become quite tuned in. For those with limited language skills, sight, sound, touch, taste and that indefinable something which I shall call 'intuition' are all important channels of communication alongside words. Frances Young reminds us in her essay on disability, 'We are a psychosomatic whole!'[12] If we work hard at relating with people of limited communication, we will enable them to respond that little bit more to other people and then to God.

Disability and Suffering

Those who are well have no need of a physician, but those who are sick. Go and learn what this means, "I desire mercy, not sacrifice." For I have come to call

---

12 F Young, *Face to Face* (T and T Clark, 1990), p 191.

not the righteous but sinners' (Matthew 9.12-13).

Psychologist Robin Skynner, in dialogue with John Cleese (of Basil Fawlty fame!) in their book *Life and How to Survive It* says, 'It's easy enough to understand what "normal" means once you've grasped the principles by which people function at the healthy and unhealthy ends of the scale. "Normal" people are simply in between the two!'[13] I might seem 'able' until my back goes or my car breaks down. During the former I am reduced to crawling and with the latter I display acute signs of learning disability! Shyness, lack of self esteem, arrogance, phobias, selfish ambition, alcoholism, drugs, beset our society and show it as it really is—disabled. Although learning disability obviously falls in to a more innocent category of suffering than some of these other things, it does focus a common human frustration at being less than we would like to be. Thus the temptation to overlook the learning disabled is, in some cases, due to the fact that it threatens to highlight a denial of our basic human condition. A community which knows its fallenness would not collude in societies attempt to, '[simply] delegate to professionals, and hope it [learning disability] will go away.'[14]

Disability, as with all suffering, is usually the result of conflict. Conflict arises in our bodily cells, between different personalities, or even in climatic conditions. Integrating the learning disabled into our faith communities may bring conflict. Taking on board new kinds of needs may mean making some sacrifices. The Scriptures reassure us here, though, as to the fruits of an honest approach. Creation came out of chaos and the resurrection out of hopelessness. Conflict is the beginning of growth and maturity, as adolescence often proves. Giving welcome to those with learning disabilities and being prepared to risk possible conflict to achieve it is the beginning. The learning disabled disciple needs to be allowed and enabled to give of themselves as well as receiving. Facilitating this is a work of evangelism and a freeing of the potential that people have, however limited.

Releasing Captives

'The Spirit of the Lord is upon me, because he has anointed me to bring good news to the poor. He has sent me to proclaim release to the captives, and recovery of sight to the blind, to let the oppressed go free...' (Luke 4.18–20)

Jesus began his preaching by calling people to repentance (Mk 1.15). In the Greek of the New Testament *metanoeo* means literally 'to perceive afterwards.' This conveys the idea of changing one's mind or purpose. Jesus applied this to people's relationship with the Father in the parable of the Prodigal Son, who redirected his life (Luke 15.11-42). Repentance is about positive response to God— coming home. Having responded, however tentatively, we all need the affirmation of hearing Jesus say, 'Go your faith has made you well!'[15] A growing faith—whether expressed in ideas, a more loving way of being or a warm grunt—cannot help but be infectious. We need to remember that learning disabled disciples are witnesses

---

13 *Life And How To Survive It* (Methuen, 1993), p 39.
14 *Face to Face*, p 130.

for Christ too. Nobody is brought into the Kingdom of God in order to keep quiet about it. When I first darkened the doors of St Paul's Church in Nottingham a man with Down's syndrome regularly smiled and nodded at me, but never spoke. I sensed that something drew him to worship and recognized the same feeling in myself. This encouraged me to go with the flow and explore what I could not merely analyse. Many of the learning disabled tend to be less inhibited in what they do or say, and God does use this. Because the Spirit communicates on many levels of our being the learning disabled disciple has much to give, but only when we are bold enough to risk some loss of control. We cannot, for instance, control tightly when people are permitted to speak. Jesus once said to the authorities when they tried to silence his followers; 'I tell you, if these (people) were silent, the stones would shout out' (Luke 19.40).

People who live and work with the learning disabled will testify to many frustrations in relationships. That is the reality. However, one thing they will also often note is the level of openness such people often exhibit. One of the reasons for this (and there are others) is that they cannot hold so much of an overview of life. They live more from one moment to the next. This of course can be a handicap but it also means they tend to be less bound by rigid agendas. This can also mean for them that there are less barriers to the Holy Spirit. This openness is often expressed in non-verbal ways but may yet be prophetic. At my own wedding service the vicar asked our three children from previous marriages whether they approved of our union. James, who as far as we are aware did not understand the words, stepped forward, smiled and grunted loudly…coincidence or God-incidence? In an article on charismatic spirituality John Goldingay says, 'Why do we affirm the body, wholeness, healing and movement in worship, and yet see revelation as coming direct from God as though the person's body had nothing to do with it!'[16] This openness though can only flourish in the midst of a loving community.

A Sacramental Evangelism

'The church is the primary agent of mission' says Robert Warren, the Church of England's National Officer for Evangelism.[17] The church is still largely known through its local congregations. Whenever they take seriously the task of reaching the learning disabled with the gospel, they live out the church's calling to mission. In doing this, they advertise loudly and clearly the primary purpose of the church's existence, and demonstrate the profound conviction that the church is the whole people of God. The often unspoken side of this is immediately stripped away—that subtext which can so easily read, 'The sitting-still, speaking-in-the-right-place, non-dribbling, bladder-controlling people of God!' According to Paul the body of Christ cannot be complete without the weakest members—who are

---

15 Matthew 9.22; 15.28; Mark 2.5; 10.52; Luke 17.19; 18.42.
16 *Theology* (SPCK) May-June 1996.
17 R Warren *Building Missionary Congregations* (Board of Mission, 1995) p 2.

in fact quite indispensable. Indeed he insists, '…the less respectable members are treated with greater respect' (2 Cor 12.12ff). Churches which attempt to integrate people with learning disabilities have taken this principle to such extremes that they should have no problem welcoming anybody!

The worship of a local congregation expresses its identity. Styles of course vary, giving the church a richness of expression. But responding corporately to a living God, revealed in Christ, and present in the person of the Holy Spirit, is the commonality. The most common Hebrew word for worship in the OT was *abad* meaning to serve. This includes all acts of service, from awesome adoration to clearing out the donkey droppings! Likewise the most frequently occurring Greek words in the NT for worship, *latreia* and *leitourgia*, convey a similar idea. The biblical implication is that worship and service are identical twins. A church I belonged to in Nottingham, St Paul's, Wilford Hill, illustrates this relationship. Within the parish is a residential hostel and a day centre for the disabled, both physically and intellectually. On a Sunday morning an array of wheelchairs, walking frames and linked arms creates an icon to this kind of understanding of worship. The presence of learning disabled worshippers is a tangible sign of both a church's desire for its worship to ripple out into serving the wider community, and of the proclamation to the *ptochos* (the poor and underprivileged). This leads us to consider the prophetic aspect of a local church's calling under God.

The situation for learning disabled people has improved considerably in the last decade or two. However, attitudes and the degree to which people feel comfortable with unusual behaviour still lags well behind policy (as does government funding!) When I visited St Paul's, Banbury a number of the congregation had learning difficulties. They all seemed to be fairly relaxed members of that community. When people are accepted for who they are, a prophetic message is proclaimed by any church. David Jenkins wrote that 'God is about the fulfilment of being human.'[18] This is really the word of God for our culture as it emerges from an 'age of reason' and tries to rediscover what it means to be more fully human. A bonus too is that when faced with the question of, 'How can God be loving when he allows so much suffering?' a church credibly turns the question around. By living it out, it now asks, 'Why not discover how God's love can transform suffering?'

As well as pastoral caring being clearly seen, our post-denominational attitudes are also flagged up. In our ecumenical times the presence of our learning disabled friends shows a commitment to discipleship as well as simply doctrinal assent. One could go on. But it should be clear by now that seeking to introduce our learning disabled brothers and sisters to Christ and his church represents a much bigger desire. Appropriate evangelism among society's most insignificant, and most difficult to communicate with (seemingly), is an amplification of a missionary intent—that of reaching the women and men of our postmodern age, for whom any understanding of personal faith will need to be a felt as well as an

---

18 David Jenkins, *Good God!*, Lecture 4, p 3.

intellectual spirituality. Reaching learning disabled people is godly and important in itself, but the insights gained and the message promoted will enhance all
areas of a church's outreach. Moreover, under God it is an outward sign of a far
bigger inner desire—that of creating an open, welcoming, outward-looking faith
community.

Community—the Key to Belonging

'And at the end of the week Christopher Robin said, "Now!" So he took hold
of Pooh's front paws and Rabbit took hold of Christopher Robin, and all Rab-
bits friends and relations took hold of Rabbit, and they all pulled together...'

A A Milne, *Winnie-The-Pooh*

In his book *Community and Growth*, Jean Vanier observes that '...many people
live alone, crushed by their loneliness.'[19] Community is the opposite of this starv-
ing of relationship and vital to well-being. Those with learning difficulties can be
particularly vulnerable to the loneliness of being locked into their own world.
Creating community is at the heart of Christian theological tradition in the doctrine of the Trinity. Individualism, separateness, and fragmentation give way to
individuality, mutuality and belonging. If any 'member' of the Godhead ceases
to be the Trinity ceases to be! It is 'a communion of heart and spirit, a network of
relationships.'[20] When God's people reflect this interrelationship it is a nurturer of
the image of God. Community is where the learning disabled, and others, become true people, in that they give and receive. Here too we live out the signifi-
cance of the incarnation.

---

19 Jean Vanier, *Community and Growth* (DLT, 1989), p 8.
20 *ibid.*

5

Discovering God Together:
An Appropriate Evangelism

'All who believed were together and had all things in common...they broke bread at home and ate their food with glad and generous hearts, praising God and having the goodwill of all the people. And day by day the Lord added to their number those who were being saved.'

Acts 2.43-47

Drawing together the lessons of F&L and relevant theological concerns helps us to formulate an incarnational model of evangelism operating both within and from our faith communities. In practice the principles of this should be applicable to a specialized group on F&L lines or the local church in the parish. This model differs from what is often referred to as presence evangelism, being more strategic by seeking actively to facilitate response to God. The incarnational model reflects Jesus' non manipulative style by which he created the conditions for people to respond but left them to choose whether to do so.

Powerfully Simple!
'Once when the beasts were arguing among themselves as to which of the animals could produce the largest number of whelps at birth, they went to the lioness and asked her to settle the dispute.
"And how many do you have at birth?" they asked.
"One," she said defiantly, "but that one is a lion!"'
Aesop's Fables (Penguin Edition)

'Keep it simple' is a key phrase! It does not mean 'make it babyish,' 'do it quickly' or 'don't prepare properly.' My own experience is that a good ten-minute talk takes a lot more preparation than a 25-minute ramble! Simple but with great quality and, whether it is something to do, something to see or something to hear, it must be understandable—able to be received somehow. It is worth recalling three of my findings from F&L which help facilitate this.

Being Relevant
When working with those with learning disabilities we need to relate to their situation. Practically, this means getting to know people with learning disability. Everyone will have a distant cousin, or once knew someone who was 'like that,' but that may not be enough. One could become involved with some local housing scheme for the learning disabled, help at a school for those with special needs or get alongside a family where a member is learning disabled. They will wel-

come you, I almost guarantee it! As well as being educational this is part of the outreach strategy anyway, as contacts are made. F&L itself is a good place to begin as it is quite normal to be welcomed at meetings as a friend. Entering their world a little is the way to understanding how to express the gospel. For example, only when one understands the heightened importance of touch to the learning disabled person can one use it to convey the gospel simply. To touch someone's eyes as you read of the healing in Matthew 9.27-31 is powerful! Simplicity needs careful thought, and some understanding of the special needs of the other person.

Small and Very Christian

Let go of hoping for life-long commitments to Christ. Be more aware of the tiny moves that people make towards God. A smile during a song for the first time may be a step of faith. Touching someone's arm, quite deliberately during prayers may be an important new response to God's love. A scribbled picture of Jesus may give a whole new expression to someone's spirituality. These small responses are as valid as reciting a creed for someone for whom doctrine is difficult to comprehend. Affirming and encouraging all these acts of repentance can only happen within a loving Christian environment. This requires thought and structure, or chaos could happen. This is a team ministry in which every helper must know their responsibilities. A congregation too needs to be clear about what is and is not acceptable, if people are to relax during worship. Flexible structure will, paradoxically, allow spontaneity and openness to the Holy Spirit. However, task orientated people, like myself, beware. It is in the process of doing things that the learning disabled are more likely to express themselves, rather than in the completion of tasks. I shall return to this at the end of the chapter. Before that we need to look at the practicalities of communicating creatively, using all the bodily senses. That way our learning disabled friends can really hear the gospel.

Sight, Sound and Smell

Lots of colourful pictures to illustrate stories are always worthwhile. At many special needs schools they place great emphasis on the use of photographs, even to the point of photographing the toilet! Likewise for worship it is helpful being very 'catholic' and visual with some kind of focus. This of course can be done in an evangelical way just as easily! Candles, things people have collected like shells, stones, pictures, crosses or whatever can be used. Icons have been described as 'representations of the truth.' The more icons, with a small 'i,' we create the better. Ideally the whole room/church needs to be the icon. A grant from a local authority or charity and a community service team can sometimes spruce up a place with a lick of paint. Make sure the windows are clean and the flowers colourful, get in touch with what the place feels like. Finally use the Makaton sign language as much as you are able. For those living in residential homes or attending centres, it will be something they will be used to seeing. It is particularly powerful when used with songs and gives them an extra dimension. Imagine taking the gospel message to a remote tribe in the Amazon jungle. Probably one of the first things we would do is set about translating the Bible into their language! With regard to music, recent controversies over subliminal messages in popular records highlights how subtle this form of communication is. Whilst we avoid manipulation, we can use it more creatively (for example, in creating the mood of a story, be it happy, sad, dramatic or whatever). Likewise drama can be enhanced with sound effects, sometimes the funnier the better. It is amazing how funny a sneeze can be, communicating on many levels! Whilst on the subject of noses, scented candles can add something to a setting too. If one were to use a similar smell regularly it might be associated with the fact that it is time to 'pray to Jesus.' Smells are stored in the memory as readily as facts.

Drama, Touch and Prayer

Drama holds the attention for much longer than talking alone. It combines many things as life is acted out in front of us. It also gets across stories in imaginative ways, without necessarily explaining everything. Parables are capable of dying a sudden death when explained! Role playing is merely an extension of the sacraments; things stick once we do them. Putting bandages on each other to be a good Samaritan is memorable, even if the story cannot be remembered. Struggling up front to try and express prayers is intercession in itself, even if you cannot spell the word! Appropriate touch, too, can be a powerful communicator and often important where words are of more limited use. Avoid the extremes. A lack of physical touch only reinforces isolation, whereas the charismatic hug can be invasive, especially if you are a big person. To have someone gently take your hand, and tell you that Jesus loves you, can be very powerful. This is especially so for those who accept it without analysis. Prayer too needs to be enacted, lived out. If running a specific group for the learning disabled (like F&L or a housegroup) aim for at least as many more able people as disabled. Ensure some pastoral networks are in place so that nobody goes unnoticed in times of strife. For many people caring for families in such situations seems daunting, because things cannot be made better. Ironically though, these situations are those where very simple practical assistance can mean a lot. To take someone out for a while giving them a different face to see and their carers an hour's peace can make a real difference. This could be a real contact point for churches but needs some ongoing commitment. It would not be fair to start something which was difficult to continue. Absolutely everything attempted needs saturating in Christ, a vision which does not have to be a cliché. When articulating prayers with those of limited intellectual abilities, use the name Jesus often. This is less abstract than 'God' and the less able the folk, the more important this is.

Wonder, creativity and pain—the birth of a child, a seed sprouting or the Resurrection of Christ—all touch us beyond words. Evangelism which relies less on concepts needs to cultivate this sense of wonder. Nature, new life and the amazing things Jesus does can all aid this process, without requiring deep explanation. Allow creative craft tasks to back this up. If you feel you want to produce something for others to see, then someone will need to do quite a lot beforehand. The learning disabled folk can then add the special touches. For example, produce a huge tree and then let the group/congregation cut and add the leaves and flowers with their names on—a tree of life! Wonder is closely akin to prayer itself, as the immanent Spirit connects with us. The joy which a sense of awe can nurture may often lead to an even greater openness to the Lord. It is also a balance to the suffering of disability, although the pain does need expression. Leaders who are able to show some vulnerability of their own will facilitate this more easily and free others to do the same. A safe environment in which people can share difficulties is worth working hard to create. This release of frustration is often an appropriate response to God, for both disabled and carers. The psalmist cried, 'Hear my prayer, O Lord; let my cry come unto you' (Psalm 102.2). Anyone desiring to communicate a purely 'happy clappy' faith will probably be humbled. This is life as it is; both wonderful and very, very messy!

Words and Dreams

I do not want to do away with words for conveying the gospel. All the other avenues of communication work alongside words, providing a holistic approach. This holistic approach underpins my model for evangelism among those with learning disabilities. It operates when integrated within the faith community, not as another add on. These learning disabled disciples are evangelizing us with our weaknesses, as we evangelize them. The role of the leader or evangelist is that of facilitator.

'Many people are good at talking about what they are doing, but in fact do little. Others do a lot but do not talk about it. They are the ones who make and sustain community.'

Jean Vanier, *Community and Growth* (p 263)

'As I walked through the wilderness of the world, I came to a place where there was a den. There I lay down to sleep; and as I slept I dreamed a dream.'

Opening of *Pilgrim's Progress*, John Bunyan

St Cecilia's is an imaginary church based on the good practice of a number of congregations, which I have either been a member of or visited—most particularly those of St Paul's, Wilford Hill, Nottingham, St Catherine of Siena, Sheffield, St Simon and St Jude's, Rainworth, Nottinghamshire, and St Paul's, Banbury. St Cecilia's is a fairly modern building (those with older buildings read on). A ramp runs up to the church doors which peg back securely, and there is a toilet with grab rails and space for a wheelchair. Had St Cecilia's not raised sufficient funds to build the new building, Plan B was ready. This included a level path up to the back door and a local joiner was to make a ramp. The old toilets were to be adapted as far as practical, with the advice of the local authority's Community Occupational Therapist. The locks were to be changed for ones which could be unlocked from outside in an emergency. Quite often learning disabilities are accompanied by physical limitations too, and people really feel the cold. St Cecilia's has a good heating system and so our learning disabled friends are spread reasonably around the congregation. If the heating is poor then encourage the learning disabled to the areas identified as the warmest spots. These spaces may need reserving. Some of the people who accompany those in wheelchairs stay seated during the standing parts of a service, because for some it is uncomfortable to be surrounded by folk all standing three feet above them. Personal space is also an important issue, particularly where people are known to have epilepsy or anxiety problems. Being squashed in somewhere may be difficult for them.

For people who cannot 'understand' the sermon, the building itself takes on some of the teaching role. Cecilia's has colourful banners and pictures adorning the walls, without necessarily looking like a teenager's bedroom. These are moved around and changed about every three months. This is long enough time for people to feel at home with their particular symbols, but not so long that it stops stimulating. Visual effects along with sound and smell are used extensively during worship times. People march in carrying objects relevant to the worship. Bells ring at certain times in the service and people march around the communion table adding dramatic touches here and there. Incense provides a familiar worship smell (evangelicals please read on), and nothing is ever done apologetically! Those who find it difficult to have the service explained to them need to experience with clarity what is going on. The church around the corner from St Cecilia's has adapted some of these things for their own setting, which is slightly different. Instead of processing in, people appear to the sound of a piece of familiar music. Someone then puts the cross in its place, another lights a couple of gently smelling candles, before a booming voice from the back of the church shouts 'God's people at St Cecilia's, we come together to worship the Lord.' All stand and the service begins, during which a muffled drum beat announces the gospel and also the call for response. This 'call' can be anything from Communion and renewal of promises, to personal commitments or drawing a picture of God. The point is clear; the principles of all round communication can be applied within any tradition, or style of worship, with only two tools—faith and imagination.

Chaos is always a possibility. But gagging and binding people is probably too drastic a step! Anyone who has either mild, moderate, severe or profound learning difficulties needs a friend in the congregation. This person gets to know the disabled person and is available to take steps when behaviour is really spoiling other people's worship. Think carefully before automatically assuming a relative will deal with it. It may be the case that taking that responsibility from them for an hour will be a rare blessing. Baptism and Confirmation courses can be adapted on these principles with the proper permission. A church may even have to consider tastier bread at the communion rail for some! I have given much space to discussing worship because it is an important place of discipleship of the learning disabled, who will be less averse to attending than many supposedly able people. Full-blooded atheism is unusual among those with learning disabilities—

but outreach is still vital.

Local social services departments may have details of housing projects. Day centres still welcome voluntary helpers and invitations to hold services can often follow. St Cecilia's people go in to the local hostel/housing project. They take people shopping and help with physiotherapy routines; they pray with residents and are around whilst tears, and even tantrums, flow; they stay to 'natter' about anything and even repair wheelchair punctures. A male resident, who was physically disabled, was provided with 'scribes' to do his writing. He is now a licensed evangelist himself, with an international ministry. A minibus obtained from charitable donations transports people to services and other places. The sky is the limit with imagination and care. Indeed three years ago St Cecilia's married two of its disabled members, both of whom had been introduced into the church by others. None of these things evolved without struggle though, and a letting go of a desire to tightly control events. So this then is a taster of St Cecilia's, which actually exists, albeit fragmentedly. Getting in to the right mindset and knowing others have done it before is 80% of the task.

6
Epilogue

My soul proclaims the greatness of the Lord:
my spirit rejoices in God my saviour;
for he has looked with favour on his lowly servant:
from this day all generations shall call me blessed;
The Magnificat, the Song of Mary.[21]

God uses seemingly insignificant people to promote the gospel including an ordinary, powerless young girl in Israel, and those with learning disabilities today. Graham Cray has noted, 'Postmodern people are more likely to come to faith in Christ through spiritual experience which leads to understanding of doctrine rather than through prior intellectual assent.'[22] In seeking to share the gospel with our learning disabled friends we enlarge our understanding of how to express faith in our prevailing culture. The following insights have emerged and will, I hope, enrich our missionary endeavours.

---

21 Luke 1.46–56. This version from the *Alternative Service Book*, p 64.
22 G Cray *From Here To Where?* (Board of Mission 1992), p 18.

Spirituality and Faith

All the senses and capacities of our humanity need engaging along with the gospel. The huge growth in counselling and the psychodynamic therapies shows people's desire for a move toward wholeness or Shalom. Discovering God at home, in work, in leisure, and in pain are all important aspects of our discipleship. Hunger for more comes naturally when these connections are made. A practical theology equips ordinary people in their everyday lives. Unfortunately seeker services, special events and the like are pointless, without ordinary Christians making prior 'spiritual' contacts. We need to get it the right way around! It is important to remember that abstract concepts of God are of little relevance to many learning disabled people, so F&L was forced to be more all-round in its communication of truth. This applies more broadly too. Much evangelism in recent centuries relied largely on an intellectual understanding of God. No matter how life changing our message, even non disabled nineties people want personally to experience something. If this does not happen they will not, indeed cannot, hear our message. This need for a more subjective spirituality means we have to be willing to let go of a solely doctrine-driven gospel. Working hard at nurture strategies for new Christians can be a balance. An experiential yearning has come about as our society has realized that we cannot analytically understand everything. This in turn has led to a renewed sense of wonder, which many people with learning disabilities never lost. This feeling is largely showing itself in modern environmental concerns and gives us an amazing opportunity. Biblical principles of stewardship, thanksgiving and praise of the creator are potentially on the agenda.

Simplicity and Purpose

The 'bottom line gospel' is not really that complicated. It is built on values grounded in the Christ event. It may be a gospel value to worship the Lord but not necessarily with an organ, or indeed a Graham Kendrick songbook! We need a Saviour but do we need to manipulate people into declaring what wretched sinners they are as their first response? For some people that only adds to their isolation from God. Rather let us grapple with what most effectively expresses the gospel in our life together. The recent Turnbull report on the Church of England highlighted the need for lighter, more flexible structures. This must apply locally too. I recently took part in a parish evangelism consultation in the south of England. The parish's mission structures were outlined, on a flip chart. The diagram looked like Spaghetti Junction! Robert Warren says simply, 'enough is enough.'[23] In practice this means making priorities and sticking to them. Purpose naturally follows when priorities are worked out. F&L knew this well and focused on a particular group of people. It may prove wiser to do a little well than to tinker around with a lot. The parish system's drawback is that most people in it are not Christians, and having to reach all is impossible. Far better to choose the third block of flats on Rhodesia Street, or the people who work on the industrial estate, as our next people group—those to whom we will take the love of Christ next. To do this we all need to know our patches well.

Culturally Prophetic

'Demographics can be described as the process by which we come to know who lives where, what they are like and why.'[24] As with the learning disabled so with others. Culture is always undergoing change and many thinkers are concluding that we are at a turning point in the Western world. We probably need to spend what seems a disproportionate amount of time on discerning local culture afresh. There are a number of good workbooks available to help local leaders facilitate congregational learning. This has to precede any attempt to lead people to repentance. Life long commitment to anything is becoming an alien concept. What really matters is that people are journeying nearer to God. The most difficult response I have ever made was to step through a church door. This was as strange to me, at the time, as many churchgoers entering a bookmakers. The Engel Scale, breaking the process of becoming Christian into twenty steps, is a very useful tool.[25] Rather than wishing to make a quick commitment, most people's yearnings are probably more like that of St Augustine, 'Father, I am seeking: I am hesitant and uncertain, but will you, O God, watch over each step of mine and guide me.'[26] Learning disability reminds us of our social responsibilities, and the call to be prophetic. Culturally we remain in the world, but must not absorb all of the values of the world. Christian values of faithfulness, mutuality and respect of others are becoming counter culture and yet they can enrich it. Again Robert Warren describes holding this tension as, 'engaged,' yet 'distinctive.'[27] What an exciting evangelistic challenge to us all. The lessons of the nineteenth century gird us for this challenge. As Lesslie Newbigin has said, '…books written, during the eighteenth century, to defend Christianity against (Enlightenment) attacks, just accept the assumptions of their assailants.'[28] Let it not be so for us. The gospel and culture have a dynamic relationship. The gospel ought to shape cultural values, and culture be free to shape the expression of those gospel values.

Community…Again!

Christ announced the gospel through the poor and needy. Disciples with learning disabilities have an obvious need of others, a prophetic message for society and the church. We cannot manage without one another. We live and learn together and are on a journey. Evangelism is best done collaboratively rather than by experts acting alone. The leader's role, whether formally recognised or not, is that of Eph 4 in equipping ordinary Christians so that together we 'facilitate an

24 M Robinson and D Spriggs, *Church Planting: The Training Manual* (Lynx, 1995), p 46.
25 A scale grading peoples' progressive responses to God.
26 *Confessions* XI, 17.
27 *Building Missionary Congregations*, p 53.
28 L Newbigin, *The Gospel in a Pluralist Society* (SPCK, 1989), p 3.

environment where people can respond to Christ.'[29] Only in community do people know they belong to one another and thus to God. In a society which is increasingly fragmented this may prove to be the most attractive aspect of our message. To God be glory in the church and in Christ Jesus to all generations...and may it include this one.

Bibliography

General
Cray, G, *From Here To Where? The Culture of the Nineties* (Board Of Mission, 1992)
Hansen, A & R, *Reasonable Belief* (OUP, 1982)
Moltmann, J, *The Power of the Powerless* (SCM, 1983)
McFaddyen, A, *The Call To Personhood* (CUP, 1990)
Newbigin, L, *The Gospel in a Pluralist Society* (SPCK, 1989)
Pailin, D, *A Gentle Touch* (SPCK, 1992)
Skynner, R & Cleese, J, *Life and How To Survive It* (Methuen, 1993)
Vanier, J, *Community and Growth* (Darton, Longman & Todd, Revised Edition, 1989)
Warren, R, *Building Missionary Congregations* (Board Of Mission, 1995)
Young, F, *Face to Face: A Narrative Essay in the Theology of Suffering* (T and T Clark, 1990)

Faith and Light Publications
These are available from the Faith and Light International Secretariat, 3 Rue du Laos, 75015 Paris, or from local F&L communities.
A History of Faith and Light (1985)
Deepening Our Spirituality (1991)
The Seed and the Tree (1995)

Other Publications
Goldingay, J, Article on charismatic spirituality in *Theology*, May-June 1996 (SPCK)
Church Army, *People To People: Church Army's Corporate Strategy* (1993)
Kidd, R, 'The Churches Response To Disability' in *Theology Themes*, Autumn 1994 (Northern Baptist College)

---

29 Church Army *People To People* (1993) p 39.